LUCIA DE LEIRIS

Tropical Birds
Coloring Book

DOVER PUBLICATIONS, INC.
NEW YORK

Publisher's Note

Forty-six species of birds from tropical habitats around the globe are included in this coloring book. Among them are many of the world's most colorful avians, their plumage a kaleidoscope of bright hues and exotic shapes. All the plates have been reproduced in color on the covers for your coloring convenience. For each species, the caption gives the common and scientific names and an indication of the bird's range.

Copyright © 1984 by Lucia de Leiris.
All rights reserved under Pan American and International Copyright Conventions.

Published in Canada by General Publishing Company, Ltd., 30 Lesmill Road, Don Mills, Toronto, Ontario.
Published in the United Kingdom by Constable and Company, Ltd.

Tropical Birds Coloring Book is a new work, first published by Dover Publications, Inc., in 1984.

DOVER *Pictorial Archive* SERIES

This book belongs to the Dover Pictorial Archive Series. You may use the designs and illustrations for graphics and crafts applications, free and without special permission, provided that you include no more than four in the same publication or project. (For permission for additional use, please write to Dover Publications, Inc., 31 East 2nd Street, Mineola, N.Y. 11501).
However, republication or reproduction of any illustration by any other graphic service whether it be in a book or in any other design resource is strictly prohibited.

Manufactured in the United States of America
Dover Publications, Inc., 31 East 2nd Street, Mineola, N.Y. 11501

Library of Congress Cataloging in Publication Data

De Leiris, Lucia.
  Tropical birds coloring book.

  (Dover pictorial archive series)
  Summary: Forty-four drawings, with descriptive notes, of a variety of tropical birds, which may be colored or painted.
  1. Birds—Tropics—Pictorial works. 2. Painting books. [1. Birds—Tropics. 2. Coloring books] I. Title. II. Series.
  QL695.5.D45 1984   598.29'13   84-5933
  ISBN 0-486-24743-0 (pbk.)

1. The **Keel-billed Toucan** (*Ramphastos sulfuratus*) lives in dense, low-lying jungle from Mexico to Colombia and Argentina. The long bill enables it to reach for fruit and the eggs of other birds with ease, and its bright color may serve to intimidate predators.

2. The **Hoatzin** (*Opisthocomus hoazin*) inhabits permanently flooded forest regions around the great rivers of northeastern South America, particularly the Amazon. It feeds largely on marsh plants.

3. The **Green Jay** (*Cyanocorax yncas*) ranges from Mexico to Bolivia. It is the most colorful of the jays, which are members of the crow family.

4. The **Green-tailed Sylph** (*Aglaiocercus kingi*) inhabits the Andes Range in Venezuela, Bolivia, and Peru. Like many other hummingbirds, it feeds on the nectar of flowers.

5. The **Greater Bird of Paradise** (*Paradisaea apoda*), a native of New Guinea, is known for its bright plumage, which is displayed in order to attract a female during mating season. The drab female carries out the task of nesting and raising young without assistance from her mate.

6. The **Toucan Barbet** (*Semnornis ramphastinus*) inhabits the Andes of Colombia and Ecuador. The strong bill is used for tearing fruit and crushing hard berries.

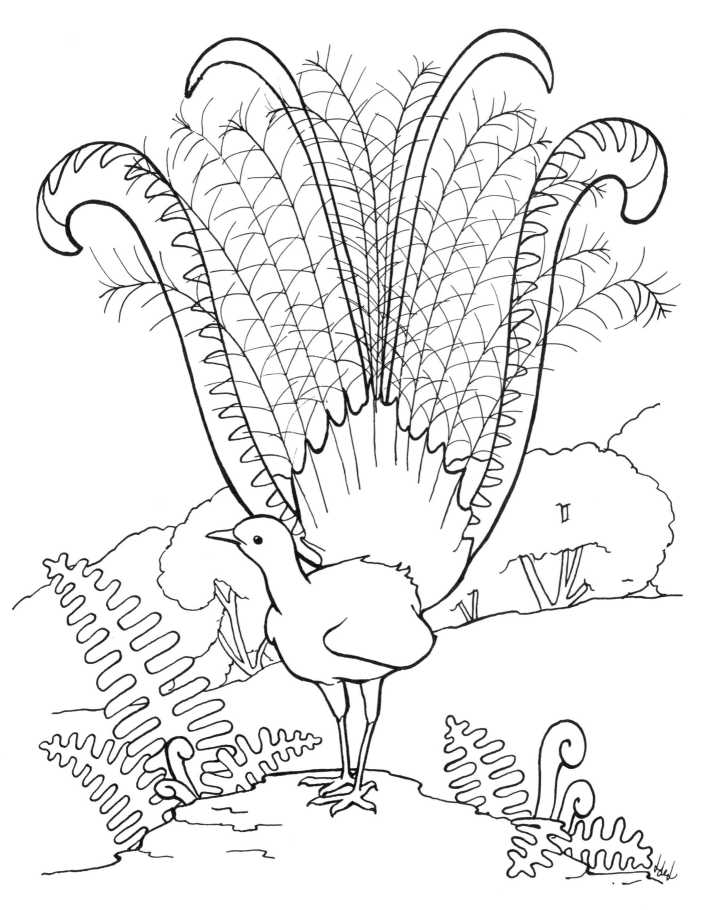

7. The **Superb Lyrebird** (*Menura novaehollandiae*) of Australia is an expert mimic of sounds, from the calls of other birds to the noise of ax-blows and the barking of dogs. The male bird scratches earth into a mound on which he sings and displays his lyre-shaped tail.

8. The **Mexican Trogon** (*Trogon mexicanus*) lives in the high mountain forests of Mexico and Central America. Insects and spiders form the bulk of its diet.

9. The **Sulfur-crested Cockatoo** (*Cacatua galerita*) is a member of the parrot family and a native of Australia and New Guinea. It dwells in rain forest, high in the trees.

10. The **Scarlet Ibis** (*Eudocimus ruber*) ranges from Venezuela to Brazil. It feeds on small animals in shallow water.

11. The **White-crested Guan** (*Penelope purpurascens*) is an arboreal bird that feeds chiefly on fruit and nuts. It ranges from southern Mexico to Venezuela and Ecuador.

12. The **Regal Sunbird** (*Cinnyris regius*) inhabits central Africa. It feeds on nectar, insects, and fruit. Two males are shown; the female lacks such bright plumage.

13. The **Tawny Frogmouth** (*Podargus strigoides*) lives in Australian and Tasmanian woodland. It feeds mainly on arthropods, using its beak to strike its prey.

14. The **Common Peafowl** (*Pavo cristatus*), native to India and Sri Lanka, is a member of the pheasant family. The broad, iridescent tail is more than twice as long as the body.

15. The **Magnificent Frigate-bird** (*Fregata magnificens*) occurs on both coasts of Central America, generally breeding on islands. It ranges far out to sea, catching fish and squid as well as stealing food from other seabirds. The female is shown above, the male below.

16. The **Red-collared Lorikeet** (*Trichoglossus haemotodus rubritorquis*), a member of the parrot family, ranges from the East Indies to Australia and the New Hebrides.

17. The **Green Magpie** (*Cissa chinensis*) is found from the Himalayas to Southeast Asia. It is a member of the crow family.

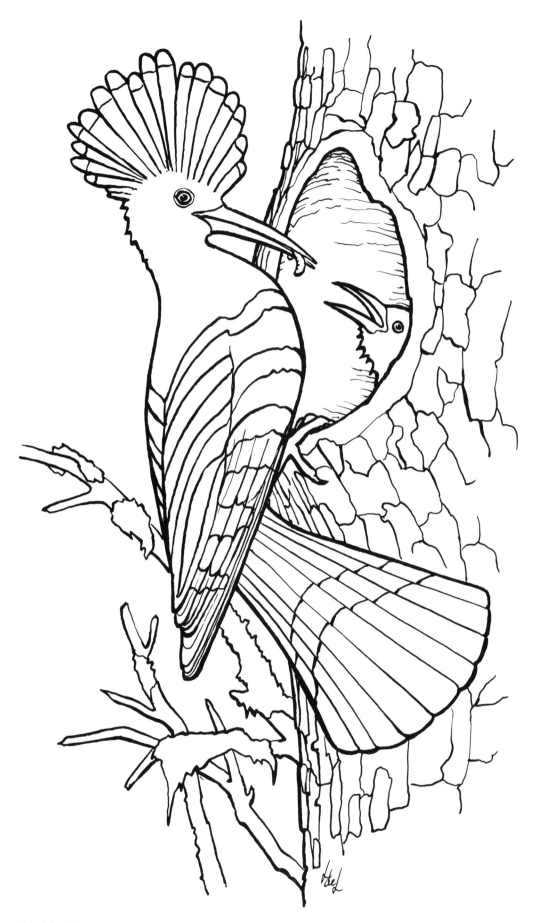

18. The **Hoopoe** (*Upupa epops*) is widely distributed on the Eurasian land mass, and is also found in Africa. A bird of myth and folklore, it figures in Classical literatures and was the basis for an Egyptian hieroglyph.

19. The **Lilac-breasted Roller** (*Coracias caudata*) lives in the lowlands of tropical Africa. Rollers are so named because of their habit of doing loops and somersaults during display flights.

20. **The Guianan (or Common) Cock-of-the-Rock** (*Rupicola rupicola*) is a native of northeastern South America. The brilliant orange plumage of the male attracts the dull, earth-brown female during courting.

21. The **Turquoise-browed Motmot** (*Eumomota superciliosa*) is found from Mexico to Costa Rica. It feeds largely on insects, returning to its perch with its prey and beating it ferociously against the branch.

22. The **Roseate Spoonbill** (*Ajaia ajaia*) ranges from the southeastern U.S. and the West Indies to Argentina and Chile. It feeds by waving its open bill back and forth in shallow water. The bill snaps shut when touched on the inside by floating water animals.

23. The **Rhinoceros Hornbill** (*Buceros rhinoceros*) is a Malaysian bird. The female, as shown here, walls herself up in the nest cavity and depends on the male for food while brooding.

24. The **Paradise Flycatcher** (*Terpsiphone paradisi*), which inhabits much of Asia, is an insectivore as its name implies, often catching insects on the wing. Its plumage has a red and a white phase, both of which are shown here.

25. The **Double-wattled Cassowary** (*Casuarius casuarius*) is a six-foot-tall, flightless bird, inhabiting the dense undergrowth of rain forest in northern Australia and New Guinea. It has adapted to its surroundings by developing coarse, hairlike feathers not easily damaged by vegetation, and a casque that protects the head as it moves through the undergrowth.

26. The **Satin Bowerbird** (*Ptilonorhynchus violaceus*) is a native of Australia. Like other bowerbirds, it builds a bower of plant material and decorates it with leaves and berries to attract its mate.

27. The **Pink-breasted Paradise Kingfisher** (*Tanysiptera nympha*) is a rare inhabitant of New Guinea. Like other kingfishers, it dives for fish and other aquatic prey.

28. The **Rufous-breasted Wren** (*Thryothorus rutilus*) inhabits central and northern South America. Like other wrens, it feeds chiefly on insects.

29. The **Village Weaver** (*Ploceus cucullatus*) is a native of Africa. Village Weavers may suspend a large number of woven nests from the twigs of a single tree.

30. The **Mandarin Duck** (*Aix galericulata*) is a mostly vegetarian inhabitant of east Asia. In the Chinese tradition it is considered a model of conjugal fidelity.

31. The **Quetzal** (*Pharomachrus mocino*) ranges from southern Mexico to Costa Rica. It was the sacred bird of the ancient Maya and Aztec civilizations.

32. The **Caribbean Flamingo** (*Phoenicopterus ruber ruber*) occurs in the West Indies, with another population in the Galápagos Islands. Flamingoes nest in colonies, building nests of mud and stones in which each pair lays a single egg.

33. The **Fairy Bluebird** (*Irena puella*) ranges from India to Indochina and the East Indies. It feeds on the pulp of tropical fruit and on insects.

34. The **Crowned Pigeon** (*Goura cristata*) is the largest of the pigeons. It inhabits New Guinea and some neighboring islands.

35. Macaws are forest dwellers and the largest members of the parrot family. The **Scarlet Macaw** (*Ara macao*) on the left ranges from Mexico to Bolivia, the **Blue and Yellow Macaw** (*Ara ararauna*) on the right from Panama to Argentina.

36. The **Iiwi** (*Vestiaria coccinea*) is one of the Hawaiian honeycreepers, a varied family of small birds that illustrates specialized adaptation to differing food supplies. The Iiwi's curved beak is adapted to feeding on the nectar of flowers.

37. The **King Vulture** (*Sarcoramphus papa*) ranges from southern Mexico to Argentina. It feeds on snakes and carrion in woods near marshes and rivers.

38. The **Blue Bird of Paradise** (*Paradisaea rudolphi*), shown here in courtship display (above), is a native of New Guinea.

39. The **Sunbittern** (*Eurypyga helias*) ranges from southern Mexico to Peru, Bolivia, and Brazil. Found mostly on the larger rivers, it feeds on insects, small crustaceans, and tiny fish.

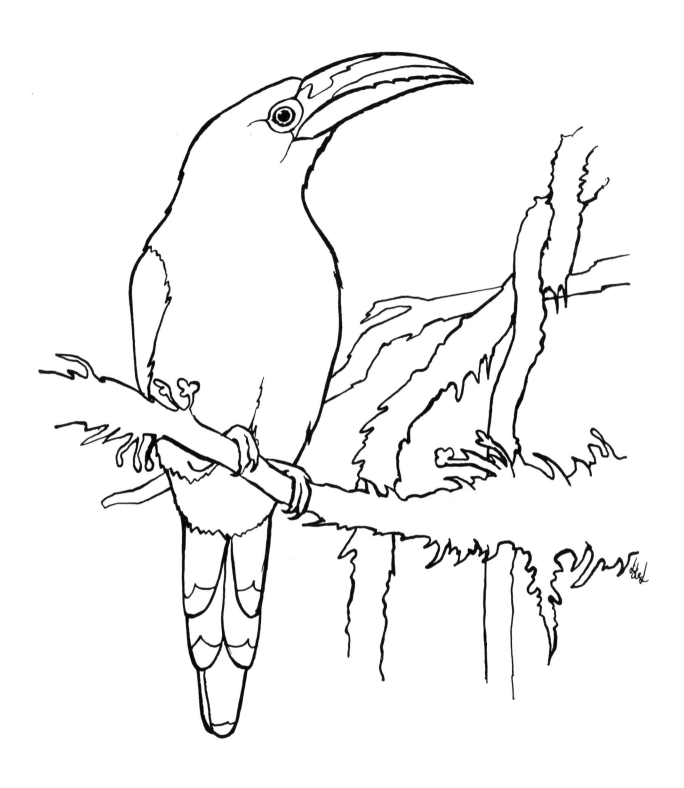

40. The **Emerald Toucanet** (*Aulacorhynchus prasinus*) lives in mountain forests from Mexico to Peru.

41. The **Black-eared Golden Tanager** (*Tangara arthus*), shown on top, lives in mountainous regions from Venezuela to Bolivia; the **Flame-crowned Tanager** (*Tangara parzudakii*) at bottom ranges from Venezuela to Peru. Tanagers are largely fruit eaters, but also include some insects in their diet.

42. The **King Bird of Paradise** (*Cicinnurus regius*) is the smallest of the birds of paradise. Like the others, it is known for its display of bright plumage during mating season. It is a native of New Guinea.

43. The **Copper-rumped Hummingbird** (*Amazilia tobaci*) inhabits Venezuela and Trinidad and Tobago. It is one of over three hundred species of hummingbirds.

44. The **Garnet Pitta** (*Pitta granatina*) lives in the forests of Malaya, Sumatra, and Borneo, where it feeds on small terrestrial animals.

Index of Common and Scientific Names

DOVER COLORING BOOKS

Paperbound unless otherwise indicated. Prices subject to change without notice. Available at your book dealer or write for free catalogs to Dover Publications, Inc., 31 East 2nd Street, Mineola, N.Y. 11501. Please indicate field of interest. Each year Dover publishes over 300 books on fine art, music, crafts and needlework, antiques, languages, literature, children's books, chess, cookery, nature, anthropology, science, mathematics, and other areas.

Manufactured in the U.S.A.